....LEARN PUBLIC SPEAKING IN....
10 MINUTES OR LESS

....LEARN PUBLIC SPEAKING IN....
10 MINUTES OR LESS

DR. ISAAC USOROH

TATE PUBLISHING
AND ENTERPRISES, LLC

Published by Tate Publishing & Enterprises, LLC
127 E. Trade Center Terrace | Mustang, Oklahoma 73064 USA
1.888.361.9473 | www.tatepublishing.com

Tate Publishing is committed to excellence in the publishing industry. The company reflects the philosophy established by the founders, based on Psalm 68:11,
"The Lord gave the word and great was the company of those who published it."

Book design copyright © 2015 by Tate Publishing, LLC. All rights reserved.
Cover design by Nino Carlo Suico
Interior design by Shieldon Alcasid

Published in the United States of America

ISBN: 978-1-68207-037-6
1. Self-Help / General
2. Self-Help / Personal Growth / General
15.09.11

CONTENTS

PREFACE

The way you prepare and write your speech will take a new turn. This book will introduce you to a much easier, simple, creative, efficient, and effective way of preparing, writing and presenting your speech. This book has the inside scoop. You are invited to explore the essentials strategies of becoming a competent and effective public speaker.

PROGRESSION

This book is carefully prepared to satisfy the following needs:

- ❖ Understand the different essential elements involved in preparing and presenting your speech.
- ❖ Provide an opportunity of understanding the dynamics of speech delivery
- ❖ Explore the principles and guidelines of effective speech presentation.
- ❖ Bridge the distance between your speech goal and its accomplishment.

OVERVIEW

We will cover the following topics and materials in this book

- Carefully understand the importance of the audience.
- Carefully understand how to analyze the audience.
- Take into consideration the importance of the venue of our speech.
- Adequately understand how to develop a speech topic
- What, where, when, and how to get information.
- How to organize our information
- How to adequately cite information
- Recognize various ways to support our speech
- Identify the best way to present our speech

This book also includes activities that will gradually guide you through the process of developing your speech. It will also show you simple ways to present your speech.

I sincerely hope this book is useful in satisfying your quest. Please let me know what you think so that I can better assist you, and make future editions more useful.

Isaac Usoroh
Savylearn
Isaac@savylearn.com

1

UNDERSTANDING
THE AUDIENCE

UNDERSTANDING YOUR AUDIENCE

THE AUDIENCE

"Experience is the name everyone gives to their mistakes"

—OSCAR WILDE

The process of writing or preparing a speech is a tedious one. I'm sure you are probably rambling through prospective topics and it isn't getting any easy. You are probably telling yourself "This is not going to work". You see; this is normal. You are not going crazy. Every public speaker goes through the same phase. You wonder what to talk about, which topic is appropriate, how to present it, why you need to change a topic and more. The confusion never ends. It's like a vicious circle. Well, there is hope for you.

In this chapter we will extensively discuss the first vital point to consider before thinking about the topic of your speech. According to The American Heritage College Dictionary 3rd edition, audience is simply those assembled at a performance... an opportunity to be heard or to express one's views.

Anyone preparing any speech must first understand the dynamics of the audience. This means, you must be able to identify the needs and wants of your audience. Remember, your audience determines your speech.

Your audience is not just a gathering of people, its much more complex than that. Your audience structure is a combination of several elements. Some of these elements are the age, culture, economic status, gender, language, education, and religious beliefs of your audience. Understanding the dynamics of your audience will help you realize the foundation of your speech.

Let's consider some of these dynamics and their importance to your speech.

AGE

The age group of your audience will greatly influence the type of information you decide to present. You don't want to present a topic such as "How to save money on a new twelve bedroom home" to an audience comprised of 3 year olds. You will confuse them. Kids at that age group will rather be watching Sesame Street.

CONSIDER THIS

Why do you have to consider the age of your audience?

AUDIENCE AGE ACTIVITY 1.0

For the following age groups, write a topic that you think will be appropriate for them. For this activity, you will need to write a speech topic for each age group and answer a series of questions.

I.   AGE GROUP "A" 3 – 6 YEARS

        SPEECH TOPIC:

II.   AGE GROUP "B" 8 – 6 YEARS

        SPEECH TOPIC:

III.   AGE GROUP "C" 18 – 23 YEARS

        SPEECH TOPIC:

IV.   AGE GROUP "D" 25 – 38 YEARS

        SPEECH TOPIC:

V.   AGE GROUP "E" 40 – 55 YEARS

        SPEECH TOPIC:

VI.   AGE GROUP "F" 57 – 83 YEARS

        SPEECH TOPIC:

ANSWER THE FOLLOWING QUESTIONS

A. What challenges did you encounter while trying to choose a topic for each age group?

B. What strategy did you use to choose each topic for each age group?

C. What influenced the way you chose the topic for each age group?

D. Choose an age group, and write four main ideas you will discuss on the topic you chose for that age group.

ECONOMIC STATUS

When considering the economic status of your audience, you must ask yourself the following questions: "How rich or wealthy is my audience", "What can or can't they afford". You may not be able to accurately determine the answers to these questions but you must have an idea about them.

Just like the age element, the economic status of your audience will help you better understand your audience and a lot more about your speech.

SUPPOSE YOU WERE ASKED TO PRESENT A SPEECH TO AN AUDIENCE OF CORPORATE AMERICA CEO'S. WHAT WILL BE YOUR TOPIC AND WHAT WILL YOU DISCUSS IN YOUR SPEECH?

AUDIENCE CULTURE

Culture affects every facet of our communication with others. Culture may as well refer to beliefs, norms and attitudes that are used to guide our behaviors and to solve human problems (Chen and Starosta, 1998). The culture of your audience will definitely affect the choice of information you are willing to present to your audience. Different cultures perceive and interpret information and behaviors differently. In the United States of America, you are expected to maintain high level of eye contact when engaged in a conversation. It shows you are confident. In other cultures such as one found in Japan, you are not expected to maintain high level of eye contact. This behavior may be interpreted as a form of disrespect in this culture.

Andersen (1994) effectively distinguished cultural variations using different dimensions. One of the dimensions he listed was individualism vs. collectivism. Chen and Starosta (1998) stated that "the dimensions of individualism and collectivism describes the relationship the individual and the group to which the person belongs". They further stated the following, "People in an individualistic culture tend to emphasize their self-concept in terms of self-esteem, self-identity, self-awareness, self-image, and self-expression. Personal goals supersede group goals, and competition is often encouraged in this culture". Now remember; if your audience culture is individualistic, you will have to fine-tune your speech to respond to the culture of your audience.[1]

Chen and Starosta (1998) also pointed out "Collectivistic cultures are characterized by a more rigid social framework in which self-concept plays a less significant role in social interactions".

They further explained, "In these cultures people are also expected to be interdependent and show conformity to the group's norms and values". Collectivistic cultures place more emphasis on group. Group goals supersede individual goals. As a public speaker, you must understand these dynamics. An example of individualistic culture is the America and an example of a collectivistic culture is Japan.

I assure you, after reading this book, you will have a topic for your speech, you will understand the dynamics of speech preparation and presentation, and you will become a better-informed speaker.

---

[1] Anderson. P. A (1994) Explaining intercultural differences in non-verbal communication. In L.A. Samovar & R. E. Porter (Eds.), Intercultural Communication: A reader (pp.229-239). Belmont, C A; Wadsworth.

Guo-Ming Chen and William J. Starosta (1998) Foundations of intercultural communication. Needham Height, Mass.

Why should a public speaker be adequately prepared before presenting any speech?

Use the following pictures to create a story. Be very creative

WRITE YOUR STORY HERE:

ANALYZE YOUR AUDIENCE

Conduct an audience analysis by answering the following questions

a) Who is my audience?

b) What are the characteristics of my audience?

c) What are my audience interests?

d) What seems to be common among my audience?

e) Is this an informative speech?

f) Is this a persuasive speech?

g) Is this a speech to entertain?

h) What is the cultural orientation of my audience?

i) Audience gender?

j) What is the duration of the speech?

k) What topic or subject matter did you choose?

l) Why did you choose the above topic or subject?

m) Is my topic or subject appropriate?

n) Why is it appropriate or why not appropriate?

2

THE LOCATION
FACTOR

THE LOCATION FACTOR

 The event location, building appearance, seating arrangements, time of event, occasion, and dress code are vital factors that affect the success of your speech. Each element plays an intrinsic part in the overall evaluation of your presentation. To fully understand how important these elements are to your speech, we will begin by describing the essentials of these factors.

EVENT LOCATION

The event location is simply the physical building or place where you will present your speech. As a public speaker, you really want to consider the type of multimedia technology equipment available to you. Some buildings are not equipped with certain technology capabilities.

During your speech for instance, you may need to use the Internet and the location of your event does not have Internet connection. You should always call in advance to find out the technology capabilities of your event location. Always arrive an hour early to test your equipment and use of technology before your audience arrives.

SEATING ARRANGEMENTS

 Every speech occasion has a type of seating arrangement. It is very vital that you know the type of arrangement for the occasion and you adapt yourself to the seating arrangement. The seating arrangement at a church program will be different from a seating arrangement at a stadium for football game. Whenever you are asked to present a speech at any occasion, you must consider the seating arrangements. Understanding the seating arrangement at your speech event will help you fine-tune the type of interaction activity you may wish to include during your speech.

TIME OF EVENT

The time of event is simply the time of day, length of your speech, length of the program you've been asked to present, where in the program you will be presenting. You want to really take into consideration what time of the day you will be presenting your speech. For example if your speech takes place in the day, evening, or late into the night, your audience mood and expectation can be affected.

You have to take into consideration the length of the program you've been invited to present your speech. This information will help you determine the length of your speech. A lengthy program does not beckon a lengthy speech. You want to keep it short, simple, and straight to the point. Another intricate part of this element is to understanding that your speech is a part of a whole program. It is expected that the audience would have been exposed to other activities before they listen to your speech. If they are already worn out before you present your speech, you may have a problem. Always make sure you adapt your speech to the time of event.

OCCASION

The occasion determines the type of speech you will be presenting. You don't want to present a speech with a death theme at a wedding ceremony. You want to present appropriate information that correlates the occasion. Every occasion has its theme and you want to stick to the theme as much as possible. Always find out in advance the theme of the occasion of your speech. Sometimes the theme is stated and sometimes inferred. You must stick to the theme at all times.

DRESS CODE

The dress code is the type of attire or self-presentation expected at your speech event. Every speech event has a dress code. The way you dress to bed at night is different from the way you dress to go to work. The way you dress to watch a football game at a stadium is different from the way you dressed or will dress for your wedding ceremony. The way we dress for our speech greatly influences the way the audience will perceive our presentation. For instance, suppose you are invited to present a speech at the congress to congressmen and women. I am sure you will not wear your pajama to present your speech. There is always a dress code and it can help your credibility as a speaker. Always dress to the theme of the occasion of your speech.

WHAT HAVE YOU LEARNED SO FAR? LIST ANY
FIVE MAJOR POINTS YOU HAVE DISCOVERED IN
CHAPTER TWO

3

DEVELOPING YOUR
TOPIC

DEVELOPING YOUR TOPIC

In this chapter we will discuss simple steps you can use to develop a topic for your speech. We already have a conclusive idea why the audience is essential to our speech; we also understand why the location of our speech is vital. Now, based on these assumptions lets develop our topic.

REMEMBER TO CONSIDER YOUR AUDIENCE

Your audience plays a vital role in determining your topic. You want to choose a topic that will be appropriate to them. You don't want to sound out of place when you are presenting your speech. If you have an audience composed of lawyers, you want to present information that is relevant to them. The next step will be to consider information that will be relevant to your audience.

CONSIDER SUBJECT MATTER

Considering subject matter simply means thinking about information themes that will suit you audience. The first step in achieving this goal is to consider your experience and talents. Your experience and talents can provide a wealth of information on countless information themes you can talk about. For instance, if you have military experience, you can talk about a theme such as determination and physical endurance. If you are a parent, you can talk about parenting. Now that you have several themes you can talk about, you want to consider the relevancy and timeliness of your information. You desire to choose a topic that you are excited about and in which your audience will be interested. Each theme can generate many topics. For instance, let's consider the theme "Education". You can generate several topics from this theme e.g. certification, degree, school loans, scholarships, study tips, teaching, schooling, learning, edification and more.

Let's consider another theme "Jobs". You can generate the following topics: instructor, policeman or woman, judge, profession, career management, career counseling, interviewing, job culture, job expectation, job search, coworker, associate, partner etc. Remember each theme generates topics. You should establish a technique you can use to remember those topics you would be interested in presenting. Your technique might be to simply write them down.

CONSIDER YOUR SPEECH OBJECTIVE

At this stage we assume you have selected a topic for your speech and now you need to determine your speech goal. Your speech goal is simply what you want your audience to know or do at the end of your speech. After you have selected a topic, you now determine the information you wish to share with your audience. You must always take into consideration the relevancy and importance of the information you wish to share with your audience. Remember if it is not relevant to your audience, they will not listen.

choose a topic

for each audience

and write

a general and specifc goal

AUDIENCE: POLICE OFFICERS

General Goal _____

Specific Goal _____

Thesis Statement _____

_____

_____

Introduction:

Body:

Conclusion:

Work Cited:

AUDIENCE: LAWYERS

General Goal _____

Specific Goal _____

Thesis Statement _____

_____

_____

Introduction:

Body:

Conclusion:

Work Cited:

AUDIENCE: PARENT TEACHERS ASSOCIATION MEETING

General Goal _____

Specific Goal _____

Thesis Statement _____

_____

_____

Introduction:

Body:

Conclusion:

Work Cited:

AUDIENCE: COLLEGE STUDENTS

General Goal _____

Specific Goal _____

Thesis Statement _____

_____

_____

Introduction:

Body:

Conclusion:

Works Cited:

AUDIENCE: CONGRESS

General Goal _____

Specific Goal _____

Thesis Statement _____

_____

_____

Introduction:

Body:

Conclusion:

Works Cited:

AUDIENCE: WHITE HOUSE EMPLOYEES

General Goal _____

Specific Goal _____

Thesis Statement _____

_____

_____

Introduction:

Body:

Conclusion:

Works Cited:

AUDIENCE: MIAMI DOLPHINS FANS

General Goal _____

Specific Goal _____

Thesis Statement _____

_____

_____

Introduction:

Body:

Conclusion:

Work Cited:

4

PLANNING YOUR
RESEARCH

===

PLANNING YOUR RESEARCH

 This is the stage where you determine the type of information you wish to use in your speech and where to get the information. The information you wish to use in your speech is greatly affected by the topic of your speech. If your speech will rely more on statistics, then, you need to perform more statistical based research. However, in public speaking, every speech topic varies on the type of research needed to gather information for that topic.

SOURCES OF INFORMATION

We assume by now you have a topic, you've determined what type of information you'll need for your topic; now let's find out where you can get the information you need.

In today's society, information gathering is made easy. The advent of technology has created a superhighway for information collection.

You can get information on the topic of your speech from the library, Internet, Government non-classified publications, interviews, personal experience, etc.

THE LIBRARY

The library holds tons of information. You have books, periodicals, articles, references, library electronic databases, encyclopedias, newspapers, and journals. The library is your one stop place to get most of the information you need for your research. However the library is not the only place to gather information for your topic.

THE INTERNET

The Internet also holds millions of electronic collection of information. All you need is access by an Internet service provider and you are ready to gather your needed information. There are countless websites online that provide free information and you can research your topic by simply typing in your topic. You can even generate ideas by typing in your topic on any of the various search engines such as, www.Ask.com, Google, MSN, Yahoo, InfoSeek and other popular sites.

INTERVIEWS

Interviews are another source for information. You can gather information by simply asking expert questions that is related to your topic. The expert response becomes a good source for your information. You have to make sure that your expert is credible for the type of information you need. For instance, you don't want to interview a Muslim cleric on the traditions of Buddhism. Also remember, your questions must be organized and carefully constructed to generate enough information regarding your topic.

GOVERNMENT NON-CLASSIFIED DOCUMENTS

These are documents that the government reckon safe for public access. You can get access to such documents through your local government department. For example, you might need statistical information on the population growth of a county for your speech. Your local government agency that deals with the issue will provide you with the needed information.

PERSONAL EXPERIENCE

In addition to electronic and printed materials, another good source for information is you. Your personal experience can provide extensive information for your topic. If your topic needs information that you already know, then, your personal experience becomes the most credible source. For instance, if you have a topic that seeks to inform your audience on the benefits of experiencing military life, your military service experience will act as a good source of information for your topic.

HOW TO CITE OR REFERENCE YOUR INFORMATION

Referencing your source appropriately is as important as your speech itself. It shows your audience that you are a credible speaker. Preparing your speech involves writing your sources so that you can cite them during delivery. In this section of the book, we will discuss extensively how to document your sources using the MLA and APA styles.

MLA STYLE

MLA stands for Modern Language Association. This association publishes the MLA handbook for writers of research papers. The following documentation format reflects the MLA style is adapted from The Little Brown Compact Handbook, revised custom edition by Jane E. Aaron.

AUTHOR NOT NAMED IN YOUR TEXT

One researcher concludes "women impose a distinctive construction on moral problems, seeking moral dilemmas in terms of conflicting responsibilities" (Gilligan 105).

AUTHOR NAMED IN YOUR TEXT

One researcher, Carol Gilligan, concludes "women impose a distinctive construction on moral problems, seeing moral dilemmas in terms of conflicting responsibilities" (105).

A WORK WITH TWO OR THREE AUTHORS

As Frieden and Sagalyn observe, "the poor and the minorities were the leading victims of highway and renewal programs"(29).

One text discusses the "ethical dilemmas in public relations practice" (Wilcox, Ault, and Agee 125).

A MULTIVOLUME WORK

After issuing the Emancipation Proclamation, Lincoln said, "What I did, I did after very full deliberations, and under a very heavy and solemn sense of responsibility"(5:438).

A WORK BY AN AUTHOR OF TWO OR MORE WORKS

At about age seven, most children begin to use appropriate gestures to reinforce their stories (Gardner, Arts 144-45).

AN ANONYMOUS WORK

One article notes that a death-row inmate may demand his own execution to achieve a fleeting notoriety ("Rights").

A GOVERNMENT PUBLICATION

A 1996 report by the Hawaii Department of Education predicts an increase in enrollments (6).

A LITERARY WORK (E.G. NOVEL, PLAYS, POEM ETC)

Novel: page number comes first, semicolon and part or chapter of work:

Toward the end of James's novel Maggie suddenly feels "the thick breath of the definite—which was the intimate, the immediate, the familiar, as she hadn't had them for so long"(535; pt.6, ch. 41).

Poem: that are not divided into parts, you can omit the page number and supply the line number(s) for the quotation. To prevent confusion with page numbers, precede the number(s) with "line(s)" in the first citation; then just use the number(s).

In Shakespeare's Sonnet 73 the speaker identifies with the tress of late autumn, "Bare ruined choirs, where late the sweet birds sang" (line4). "In me"," Shakespeare writes,"thou seest the glowing of such fire / That on the ashes of his youth doth lie"(9-10).

Plays and Poems with divided parts, omit a page number and cite the appropriate part-act…

Later in King Lear Shakespeare has the disguised Edger say," the prince of darkness is a gentleman" (3.4.147)

THE BIBLE

According to the Bible, at Babel God "did…confound the language of all the earth" (Gen. 11.9)

AN ELECTRONIC SOURCE

Business forecasts for the fourth quarter tended to be optimistic (White 4)

HOW TO CREATE THE LIST OF WORKS CITED

BOOKS

Gilligan, Carol. In a different Voice: Psychological Theory and Women's Development. Cambridge: Harvard UP, 1982

A BOOK WITH TWO OR THREE AUTHORS

Frieden, Bernard J., and Lynne B. Sagalyn. Downtown, Inc.: How America Rebuilds Cities. Cambridge: MIT, 1989.

A BOOK WITH MORE THAN THREE AUTHORS

Lopez, Roberts S., et al. Civilizations: Western and World. Boston: Little, 1975.

TWO OR MORE WORKS BY THE SAME AUTHOR(S)

Gardner, Howard. The Arts and Human Development. New York: Wiley, 1973.
—. The Quest for Mind: Piaget, Levi-Strauss, and the Structuralist Movement. New York: Knopf, 1973

A BOOK WITH AN EDITOR

Ruitenbeek, Hendrick, ed. Freud as We Knew Him. Detroit: Wayne State UP, 1973

A BOOK WITH AN AUTHOR AND AN EDITOR

Melville, Herman. The Confidence Man: His Masquerade. Ed. Hershel Parker. New York: Norton, 1971.

A TRANSLATION

Alighieri, Dante. The Inferno. Trans. John Chardi. New York: NAL, 1971

A GOVERNMENT PUBLICATION

Stiller, Ann. Historic Preservation and Tax Incentives. US Dept. of Interior. Washington: GPO, 1996.

Hawaii. Dept. of Education. Kauai District Schools, Profile 1996-97. Honolulu: Hawaii Dept. of Education, 1996.

AN ANONYMOUS BOOK

The Dorling Kindersley World Reference Atlas. London: Dorling, 1994.

A WORK IN MORE THAN ONE SERIES

Lincoln, Abraham. The collected Works of Abraham Lincoln. Ed. Roy P. Basler. Vol. 5. New Brunswick: Rutgers UP, 1953. 8 vols.

A SIGNED ARTICLE IN A DAILY NEWSPAPER

Ramirez, Anthony. "Computer Groups Plan Standards." New York Times 14 Dec. 1993, late ed.: D5.

ELECTRONIC MAIL

Millon, Michele. Re: Grief Therapy. "Email to the author. 4 May 1997

AN ARTICLE IN AN ONLINE PERIODICAL

Palfrey, Andrew. "Choice of Mates in Identical Twins." Modern Psychology 4.1 (1996): 12 pars. 25 Feb. http://www.liasu.edu/modpsy/palfrey4 (1).htm.

DOCUMENTATION: APA STYLE

The APA documentation style is a method of citing or referencing your sources that is approved by the American Psychological Association. The following documentation style is adapted from the Publication manual of the American Psychological Association, 4th ed.

ONE WORK BY ONE AUTHOR

Rogers (1994) compared reaction times

ONE WORK BY MULTIPLE AUTHORS

Wasserstein, Zappulla, Rosen, Gerstman, and Rock (1994) found

GROUP AS AUTHORS

(Reference list entry) National Department of Defence. (2005).
    (In-text entry) National Department of Defence [NDD], 2005)

ANONYMOUS AUTHOR

The book Jungle in a boy (2004)…

A WORK WITH TWO AUTHORS

Karl and Williams (2004) established that military officers under the age of 30 perform better than their older colleagues.

AUTHORS WITH SAME SURNAME

S. A. Fries (2004) and D. E. Fries (2005) also found

LIST TWO OR MORE WORKS BY DIFFERENT AUTHORS

Several studies (Jason, 2002; Daniel, 2003; Samuel, 2004; Sangathier and Gerald, 2005)

HOW TO CREATE THE REFERENCE LIST

A BOOK WITH ONE AUTHOR

Redmond, H. (1998). Confidence speaker: the elements of public speaking. Florida: Miami.

A BOOK WITH TWO OR MORE AUTHORS

Jackson, B.F., & Gregory, U. V. (2003). Space of time. Berrien Springs: Academic Press.

A BOOK WITH AN EDITOR

Jackson, B.F., & Gregory, U. V. (Eds). (2003). Space of time. Berrien Springs: Academic Press.

AN ANONYMOUS BOOK

Merriam-Webster's collegiate dictionary (10th ed). (1993). Springfield, MA: Merriam-Webster.

AN ARTICLE IN A MAGAZINE

Javier, D. (2003, November). College: When should you start dating? Ms.., 37-39, 74.

AN ARTICLE IN A NEWSPAPER

Ramirez, A (1993, December 14). Computer group plan standards. The New York Times, p. D5.

A SOURCE ON THE WORLD WIDE WEB.

Leppik, P. (1996, January 21). The two rules of Internet security [Online]. Available:
http://www.thinck.com/insec.html

AN INTERVIEW

Brisick, W.C. (1988, July 1). [Interview with Ishmael Reed]. Publisher Weekly. 41-42.

5

SUPPORTING YOUR
SPEECH

SUPPORTING YOUR SPEECH

In this chapter, we will consider the different types of support you can employ for your speech. It is not enough that you have something to say; you need to embed it with brief illustrations, descriptions, explain your terminologies and definitions, analogies, statistics, interviews, quotations and more. These elements provide support for your speech.

BRIEF ILLUSTRATIONS

Use brief illustration to make your point vivid. According to The American Heritage College Dictionary (1993), illustration means the act of clarifying or explaining, materials used to clarify or explain. You can use stories, visuals or demonstrations to make your point vivid.

EXPLAINING YOUR TERMINOLOGIES AND DEFINITIONS

You must always endeavor to explain your terminologies during your speech. Don't always assume your audience knows all your terms. You may confuse your audience and your presentation might turn out to be an awful one. The same rule applies to definitions. Try and define every ambiguous word and term you use in your speech. It helps motivate your audience to focus on the information you are sharing.

ANALOGIES

Analogy is simply the similarity in some respects between things that are otherwise dissimilar. It is a comparison based on such similarity (American Heritage College dictionary, 1993). This means a comparison of the new to the old. Analogies can help your listeners understand unfamiliar ideas, things, and situations by showing how these matters are similar to something they already know (Steven & Susan, 2000).

STATISTICS

Statistics is the mathematics of the collection, organization, and interpretation of numerical data (American Heritage College dictionary, 1993). Here you use statistics to support your argument in your speech. People attend more to information when it is supported by statistics. It helps prove your point. Remember, your numbers must be accurate and verifiable or else you will lose your credibility as a public speaker.

INTERVIEWS, QUOTATIONS, AND EXPERT OPINION

To be able to maintain strong credibility as a public speaker, it is advisable to integrate expert opinions, quotations, and even interview responses to your speech. It always demonstrates to your audience that you are well informed and prepared for your presentation.

USING VISUAL AIDS

Another resourceful means of supporting your speech is the use of visual aid. They are practical means of maintaining audience attention and creating credibility. It is very important to use visual aid in your presentation. It helps your audience retain information of your presentation. It creates a vivid picture of your presentation to your audience.

You should carefully select the type of visual aid that fits your presentation. Some times your presentation may lay more emphasis on certain types of visual aids than others. They're several types of visual aids. Some of which are: Graphs, PowerPoint slides, Photographs, Pictures, Charts, Videotapes, Digital Video Disks, People, Models and more. Your visual aid is suppose to support your speech not destroy it. Always keep it simple and precise. Remember your audience is watching every verbal and non-verbal cue you display during your speech.

6

ORGANIZING YOUR
IDEAS

WRITING YOUR THESIS STATEMENT

Building the framework of your speech is the next stage in putting your speech together. We assume you now have a topic, your research is done, your supporting materials are ready, your visual aids are ready, and you generally have a skeletal idea of what you intend to share with your audience. To begin, we will discuss how to write your thesis statement. Your thesis statement is a sentence that outlines the specific elements of the speech supporting the goal statement. Your goal statement is what you what the audience to know or do after your speech. Therefore your thesis statement simply provides an outline that specifies the elements supporting your goal statement. For instance, if the topic of your speech is "Basketball" and your goal statement is "at the end of my speech, my audience will know the three basic skills necessary to play the game of basketball". Your thesis statement will simply identify the three basic skills. Therefore your thesis statement will be "the three basic skills necessary to play the game of basketball are passing, dribbling, and shooting the ball. The thesis statement helps you organize and fine-tune the type of information you wish to share with your audience.

Immediately after the thesis statement, you should have the introduction of your speech, the body, and then the conclusion. One simple way to organize the main body of your speech is to envisage how you would like to present your information. You should ask your self "do I want to present my information chronologically, or topically, or by show of cause and effect, or by problem and solution"?

INFORMATION ORGANIZATION STYLES

CHRONOLOGICALLY

When you present your information chronologically, you are simply presenting your information in order of time of occurrence. This method works well with how-to-do speeches. A speech that informs the audience what to do in step one before they move to step two.

TOPICALLY

Arranging your ideas topically means presenting your information using the topic order. You decide what topic you wish to deal with first.

CAUSE AND EFFECT

The cause and effect arrangement outlines the cause of a problem and later in the speech it identifies the effect of the problem.

PROBLEM AND SOLUTION

You may decide to use problem and solution arrangement.

Here you state a problem and later in your speech you provide the solution.

These different arrangement methods can help you organize your speech.

Now we assume you have a topic, a goal statement, a thesis statement, and a type of information arrangement method you wish to use to organize your information. The next step will be to put together your introduction, arrange the main points of your speech, and prepare your conclusion. This next step assumes you already have your supporting materials and your main ideas. So all you need is your introduction and your conclusion.

Why is the Audience the central focus of any speech? Write six reasons to support this claim

The audience is the central focus of any speech, because...

7

UNDERSTANDING THE DELIVERY PROCESS

UNDERSTANDING THE DELIVERY PROCESS

There are 3 major types of speech. The informative speech, persuasive speech, and speech to entertain. The informative speech is simply a speech to inform. An example of informative speech is a classroom lecture. A persuasive speech seeks to change or re-enforce the perception of the audience. There is always an appeal to action. An example of a persuasive speech is a political speech. Entertainment speech simply seeks to entertain the audience. A very good example of an entertainment speech will be an after dinner speech.

No matter what type of speech you seek to present, you must have an introduction, a body, and a conclusion.

DEVELOPING YOUR INTRODUCTION

Your introduction must seek to get and grab the attention of your audience to your speech. It must lead or navigate your audience into your speech. It must also help you create credibility as a public speaker. Your audience will decide whether to listen to you or not during your introduction. It must set the tone for your speech. If you begin your speech in a boring manner, it is most likely your audience will tune you out. If you start your introduction with exuberant energy, your audience will listen to you. Your introduction helps you create a bond with your audience. It helps you secure their attention. The most vital section of your speech is your introduction. Please make it interesting.

You can use different types of introductions for your speech. You must be creative and exciting at the same time. You can start your speech using a story, rhetorical question, personal experience, a narration, an illustration, an analogy or even a quotation. It creates excitement when you begin your speech with energy and creative comments.

DEVELOPING YOUR CONCLUSION

The conclusion of your speech plays the same role as your introduction. Your conclusion must fulfill five criteria. One, it must summarize your speech. Two, it must wrap up your speech. This is where you recap all you said in your presentation. Three, it must influence your audience to change. This means your audience must feel the necessity of your speech. They must understand the impact of your speech on their lives. Four, it must conclude your speech with a bang. Your audience must know when you are done. They should not have to guess your conclusion. Conclude with a slam. Finally, it must create a lasting impression of your speech on your audience. Your audience must be able to recall your speech.

BUILDING YOUR VOCABULARY

It is very essential that you have the command of the language before you decide to present your speech. You don't want to sound and look silly when you're presenting your speech. You need to know what words to use and their meaning. If you decide to use certain words, you must know how and when to use those words.

As previously stated your audience greatly influences the type of grammar and vocabulary you use during your presentation. If you're presenting to an audience of scholars on a particular subject, you would want to make sure that your grammar meets the standard of your audience. The following exercises will hopefully add to your vocabulary building.

LEARNING OBJECTIVES

VOCABULARY BUILDING

Provide the definitions to these words

1. Meticulous

2. Mutant

3. Pagoda

4. Ovo

5. Overdo

6. Ornate

7. Pios

8. Pismire

9. Recrudescence

Use the following words in a sentence:

Recreant _____

Startle _____

Sublimity _____

Zest _____

Chieftain _____

Chiding _____

Choleric _____

Clouting _____

Verisimilitude _____

Concupiscent _____

Congeals _____

Constellated _____

Counterfeit _____

Cozenage _____

Dane _____

Thralldom _____

Hickory _____

Genre _____

Frigate _____

Dais _____

Decorum _____

Egregiously _____

Ensue _____

Enigma _____

Euclid _____

Expatiate _____

Finery _____

Flayed _____

Laggard _____

Match the following words with the correct synonym

Fortifications

    a) accumulate

    b) reorder

    c) protection

Frigid

    a) change

    b) cold

    c) miserable

Meander

    a) pace

    b) roam

    c) charm

Fascinate

   a) shine

   b) paint gold

   c) charm

Impervious

   a) protection

   b) genius

   c) resistant

Indict

   a) shine

   b) range

   c) charge

Melancholy

   a) miserable

   b) harden

   c) resent

Glisten

   a) paint gold

   b) shine

   c) believe

Gild

  a) news

  b) paint gold

  c) paint pink

Gamut

  a) pace

  b) range

  c) bewildered

Gait

  a) pace

  b) avoid

  c) reorder

Ingenious

  a) clever

  b) mysterious

  c) unknown

Congeal

  a) make plain

  b) harden

  c) beautiful

Eschew

    a) resent

    b) avoid

    c) denial

Begrudge

    a) resent

    b) reminiscence

    c) miserable

Veritable

    a) mystery

    b) recent

    c) genuine

Nostalgia

    a) charming

    b) colorless

    c) reminiscence

Reverberate

    a) unknown

    b) resound

    c) remember

Transpose

   a) reorder

   b) repose

   c) reprimand

Articulate

   a) genius

   b) eloquent

   c) genuine

Prodigy

   a) genius

   b) genuine

   c) charm

Crèche

   a) playgroup

   b) news worthy

   c) variety

Accrue

   a) disarm

   b) accumulate

   c) clever

PLANNING THE PRESENTATION OF YOUR SPEECH

An effective approach to having a successful presentation is practice. You must practice all the time. The more practice you get, the better and more confident you become. Every public speaker needs practice to become better. Practice builds confidence and creates a positive mental mind frame towards your speech. When practicing, you should try and re-create the speech environment. You must imagine yourself presenting to your audience. You can ask a friend, a colleague, or a family member to evaluate your speech during practice. It helps you discover areas of improvement. You should also give special attention to your verbal and non-verbal cues. Remember your audience will be watching your gestures, facial expressing, body movement, your personal grooming, and much more. When practicing, you should especially practice and know your introduction and your conclusion. You should visualize your success. Focus on your message and not your fear. Give yourself a mental preparation. Always seek speaking opportunities, because it helps you build confidence. Remember the more you practice, the better you become.

During practice you can work on your speech outline. Your speech outline simply outlines the specific points you will talk about in your speech. I strongly recommend that you use a speech outline to practice your speech and eventually present your speech. It makes your presentation easy and professional. I have included samples of speech outlines and possible speech topics for your brainstorming. Speech is not only about rhetoric; it is also about how you present yourself to the world. Everyday we make mini-speeches. Seize the moment and make a lasting impression.

WRITE AN INTRODUCTION AND CONCLUSION TO THE FOLLOWING SPEECH TOPICS.

I. POLICE BRUTALITY

Introduction:

_____

_____

_____

_____

Conclusion:

_____

_____

_____

_____

II. USES OF CREDIT CARDS

Introduction:

_____

_____

_____

_____

Conclusion:

_____

_____

_____

_____

III.   SMOKING AND CANCER

Introduction:

_____

_____

_____

_____

Conclusion:

_____

_____

_____

_____

IV.   INDUSTRIAL POLUTION

Introduction:

_____

_____

_____

_____

Conclusion:

_____

_____

_____

_____

V.   SOCIAL SECURITY REFORM

Introduction:

_____

_____

_____

_____

Conclusion:

_____

_____

_____

_____

VI. CLASS ACTION LAWSUIT REFORM

Introduction:

_____

_____

_____

_____

Conclusion:

_____

_____

_____

_____

VII. CITIZENSHIP

Introduction:

_____

_____

_____

_____

Conclusion:

_____

_____

_____

_____

VIII. VACATION

Introduction:

_____

_____

_____

_____

Conclusion:

_____

_____

_____

_____

XI. COMPUTERS AND HUMAN COMMUNICATION

Introduction:

_____

_____

_____

_____

Conclusion:

_____

_____

_____

_____

X. GLOBAL IMMIGRATION

Introduction:

_____

_____

_____

_____

Conclusion:

_____

_____

_____

_____

PERONAL PRACTICE SCHEDULE

Use the personal practice schedule to effectively evaluate you presentation preparation.

Date:
Duration:
Comment

PERONAL PRACTICE SCHEDULE

Use the personal practice schedule to effectively evaluate you presentation preparation.

Date:
Duration:
Comment

PERONAL PRACTICE SCHEDULE

Use the personal practice schedule to effectively evaluate you presentation preparation.

Date:
Duration:
Comment

PERSONAL PRACTICE SCHEDULE

Use the personal practice schedule to effectively evaluate you presentation preparation.

Date:
Duration:
Comment

<u>SPEECH OUTLINE</u>

INFORMATIVE OUTLINE

Topic: Chocolate's Health Benefits

General Goal: To inform

Specific Goal: At the end of the speech the class will be able to identify the health benefits of chocolate.

Thesis Statement: The three health benefit of eating chocolate are in maintaining a healthy heart, acts as an antioxidant in the blood, and it promotes longevity.

BODY:

I. The most important health benefit in eating chocolate is in reference to the heart.

   A. Eating chocolate can endorse a healthy heart.

      1. The cocoa element act like a baby aspirin.

      2. It is used as an incentive that relieves stress.

      3. Consuming the cocoa releases the nitric oxide which leads to maintenance of blood pressure.

II. The second health benefit in eating chocolate it is in reference to the antioxidant.

   A. Eating chocolate can endorse the circulatory system.

      1. Chocolate prevents the clogging of arteries.

      2. Maintains blood vessels dilated for proper circulation.

3. It posses no cholesterol, since the product cocoa comes from plants.

III. The third health benefit in eating chocolate is the proven statistics in extending life.

    A. Eating chocolate can expand your life expectancy.

        1. Recent studies have proven the fact that chocolate could extend your life a year.

        2. Chocolate eaters have a 36% lower risk of death than those who do not eat chocolate.

        3. Even the confectionery eaters (those who consume 3 or more sweets a week) still have a 16% lower risk of death.

CONCLUSION:

Eating chocolate can enhance life, it acts as a blood protector and it can improve your heart.

SOURCES:

www.english.upenn.ed/traister/choc.htm
http://co.essortment.com/chocolatehealth_rqia.htm

Topic: How to prepare for a hurricane.

General Goal: To inform.

Specific Goal: At the end of my speech, the audience will be able to know how to prepare for a hurricane.

Thesis Statement: I want my audience to fully ward off some of the danger of hurricane if they prepare.

BODY:

I. Get your family together and plan

    A. Planning ahead.

        1. What to do about outages.

        2. How to deal with personal injuries.

        3. How to turn off the water, gas, and electricity at main switches.

        4. What to do if you have to evacuate.

        5. Where to meet and whom to contact if you get separated.

    B. Emergency contacts.

        1. Post emergency phone numbers by the telephones.

        2. Teach children how and when to call 911 for help.

        3. Take a Red Cross first aid and CPR class.

        4. Make arrangements for your pets.

II. Prepare your food supply.

    A. Getting your food supply ready.

        1. Ready-to-eat canned meats, fruits, vegetables.

        2. Canned juices, milk, and soup.

        3. Staples, including sugar, salt, pepper.

        4. High energy foods including cookies, hard candy, instant coffee and, tea.

        5. Vitamins.

        6. Foods for infants, the elderly or people on special diets.

III. Secure your property and home.

    A. Secure your belongings.

        1. Board up windows or attach storms shutters.

        2. Power may go off; make sure you have enough non-perishable food.

        3. Clean everything good, and have water minimum of 3 gallons per person

        4. Check flashlights and radios, make sure you have batteries.

        5. Check trees and shrubbery, and remove limbs that could damage your house or utility lines.

IV. Special assistance.

    A. Getting special assistance

        1. Find out any special assistance that may be available in your county.

        2. If you live in a building know clearly all emergency exits.

        3. Keep a supply of extra wheelchair batteries, oxygen, etc.

V. If your home is safe, stay put

    A. Stay put.

        1. If your house is strong you should stay inside away from any windows.

        2. Don't leave your home unless you really need to.

        3. Turn off all electrical equipment to prevent damage.

        4. Don't leave your house until it is safe to do so.

VI. What to do when the storm hits.

    A. During the storm.

        1. Monitor your radio or TV for the latest weather advisories and other emergency information.

        2. Don't use electrical appliances.

CONCLUSION:

I.   Is better to be safe than sorry.

II. The best way to stay safe when a hurricane is coming is to prepare yourself and family.

SOURCES:

Personal experience: Many years living in Florida.
Research: www.bellaonline.com/articlep/art13019.asp
http://www.ns.ec.gc.ca/weather/hurricane/hurricanes6.html

SPECIFIC GOAL: I want to inform my audience about the serious problem of stress.

INTRODUCTION:

I. Stress is unavoidable consequence of life.

II. A condition or feeling experienced when a person perceived that demand exceed the personal and social resources the individual able to mobilize.

THESIS STATEMENT: There are many ways how we get stressed. It can have negative consequences. There are management techniques to avoid stress.

BODY:

There are many ways how people got stressed.

Stress is caused because;

Oppression or problems at work

Personal problems.

Over work

Not having enough time to finish things.

Dead in the family.

Stress has negative consequences.

Negative consequences are:

Headaches

Health problems

Insomnia

High blood pressure

Heart disease

Mental illness

III. We can avoid stress.

We can use management techniques such are

Relaxation techniques

hobbies

Spend time with friends and family

Exercising. Working harmoniously with others.

CONCLUSION:

Stress is a serious problem that affects everybody. We got stress out of working to many hours, family loss, to much problem at home or just to be too lonely. But we could avoid stress.

Resources: Stress management mind tools, Internet resources. Encarta.msn/media.com

SPEECH OUTLINE

How to save about $100.00 a Month by changing how you eat.

Specific Goal: To teach the audience how they can save about $100.00 each month by changing how they eat.

INTRODUCTION:

Eating is a basic need that everyone must fulfill, how you choose to eat can save you money every month

Preparing food at home and evaluating how you eat out can also save you money every month.

BODY:

Preparing beverages at home saves money

Taking time to pre buy beverages and make them at home saves money.

Buying bottled water and bringing it to school instead of buying it from the vending machine.

Brew coffee at home

Changing the way you eat out.

Altering a few habits when you eat out can save half the $100.00.

One time a month when you eat out switch to water.

One time a month when you eat out skip desert.

Eat at restaurants where kids eat free.

The last way to save is when you grocery shop.

Using coupons and buying generic saves money

Clip four coupons each month.

Switch some products from name brand to generic.

Buy what the store has on sale.

CONCLUSION:

Taking the initiative to evaluate some of your eating habits can lead to saving money. With a little planning ahead and a few alterations to your everyday food choices can save you about $100.00 each month.

RESOURCES:

Publix Grocery Stores
St.Petersberg Times

INFORMATIVE SPEECH OUTLINE

Topic: ABCD rules for early detection of Malignant Melanoma & self examination of your moles

General Goal: To inform

Specific Goal: I want my audience to learn the ABCD rules of detecting a Malignant Melanoma when they self examine their own moles.

Introduction: Talk about what is a Malignant Melanoma, normal moles and when you usually develop moles (age)

Thesis Statement: The rules to use when self examining yourself for Malignant Melanoma are A for Asymmetry, B for Border, C for Color, and D for Diameter.

BODY:

The first rule is A for Asymmetry

Early Melanomas are asymmetrical

Asymmetrical-meaning-if you draw a line thru it neither of the halves would match.

Common moles are round and symmetrical

The second rule is B for Border

This means that the border of the mole is usually irregular and has scalloped edges.

The borders of an early Melanoma are often uneven

The third rule is C for Color

When the color of the mole is not the same through out

It can have different shades of tan, brown or black and that is usually a first sign of an early Melanoma.

The fourth rule is D for Diameter

The mole should not be bigger than that of a pencil eraser.

Early melanomas tend to grow larger than your common moles.

CONCLUSION:

Talk about how important it is to self examine your moles and see a dermatologist once a year.

SOURCE:

American Academy of Dermatology

Specific Goal: I would like my audience to be informed about the three different types of treatments for lobular and ductal carcinomas. (Breast Cancer)

Introduction: Breast cancer is very treatable if it is diagnosed in its early stages.

Thesis Statement: The three major ways of treating cancer are surgery, radiation therapy and chemotherapy.

One of the major forms of treatment for breast cancer is surgery which usually consists of a lumpectomy or a mastectomy.

A.   A lumpectomy may be performed after diagnosis.

   1.   Lumpectomies usually consist of removal of the entire tumor volume with a margin of tissue around it to ensure complete removal of the abnormal tissue.

B.   mastectomy my be performed after the diagnosis.

   1.   A mastectomy usually consists of surgical removal of the entire breast with a small margin of tissue around it.

   2.   Sometimes depending on the extent of spread, a radical mastectomy may be performed in which case the entire breast is removed along with deeper seated tissue.

After surgical removal of the tumor, radiation therapy usually follows.

> Radiation Therapy for breast cancer usually consists of two ports at two different angles to make sure that they encompass the entire breast being treated.
>
> If supraclavicular nodes(nodes right below the collar bone) are positive for disease, a third field is added to the other two.
>
> After the primary treatment is finished, a lower dose with electron radiation is used around the scar area to make sure that all microscopic tissue is irradiated.
>
> Chemotherapy is usually given at the same time as surgery and radiation therapy.
>
> Chemotherapy is the use of very strong, toxic drugs to treat the cancer systemically.

CONCLUSION:

Even though breast cancer is something very serious, it is very curable if it is diagnosed and treated early. There are modern modalities such as surgery, radiation therapy, and chemotherapy to achieve this. One only needs to ask an oncologist.

REFERENCES:

Dennis T. Leaver and Charles M. Washington: Principles and Practice of Radiation Therapy: Practical Applications, Philadelphia, 1997, Mosby.

OUTLINE FOR PERSUASIVE SPEECH

Specific goal: I want my audience to believe that protecting themselves from the sun is good for their health.

Introduction: When I was in high school they used to call me tan queen. I used to layout every weekend either at the pool or by the beach. I was your typical person that would slather on the mixture of baby oil and iodine. I felt that if I wasn't getting sun I was missing something. Shortly after high school I began working for a dermatologist and I began to see what the sun actually does to your skin and I took measures to learn how to protect my skin.

Thesis: No matter your age or skin color, you need to protect your self from the sun's powerful rays! It can cause premature aging and skin cancer.

BODY:

1: There are many myths told about the sun.

Myth 1: Skin cancer develops as part of the aging process. Well that is not true! Evidence shows that if you get sun exposure during your childhood you are more likely to get skin cancer in adulthood. Besides, more and more people in their twenties and thirties are being treated for skin cancer.

Myth 2: In order for sunlight to cause skin cancer, you must first get a sun burn. Again not true. The sun causes harm regardless if you get burned or not. The skin is like a tape recorder and remembers all of the sun you have gotten now and in the past. Just walking to and from your car you are exposing your skin to harmful rays.

Myth 3: The harm done by the sun is only temporary and the skin quickly repairs itself. Not true. The skin does repair itself of superficial changes. That's why sunburn only lasts a few days and a tan fades. But the underlying damage remains. And it will not be come apparent till about 20 to 30 years from now.

2: Another effect from the sun is premature aging.

If you notice infants have clear and unblemished skin with the exception of birthmarks. In the first few years of life, moles and freckles begin to form, particularly on the exposed parts of the body such as face, neck, arms, and legs.

As a child grows older, new spots continue to appear. Studies have shown that the number of moles and freckles produced by the skin from the sun are a critical factor in the development of some type skin cancer when the child becomes an adult.

By age 21, most people show a few signs of sun damage. At 40, virtually everyone has some wrinkling, blotching, drying, and leathering of the skin. Millions of people develop precancerous growths and skin cancers each year and it is all a final result from the sun's rays.

CONCLUSION:

It is never too late to start protecting your skin from the sun! Here are a few tips to help you get on your way to beautiful and health skin!

Tip 1: Avoid the sun from 10 a.m. to 4 p.m. At these times the sun it at its most powerful.

Tip2: Apply a sunscreen with an SPF of 30 or more. Apply it 30 min before you step outside and every 20 min while you are outside. Remember to cover all exposed areas including those most commonly missed like your ears, lips, around eyes, neck, scalp if your hair is thinning, hands, and feet.

Tip 3: Wear protective clothing, including a broad-brimmed hat, UV blocking sunglasses, and tightly woven clothes. The more tightly woven the fabrics and the darker the colors the more protection you will get.

Tip 4: Beware of unexpected exposure. Many surfaces such as, sand, and cement can reflect the rays of the sun. Sitting under the shade or an umbrella does not guarantee total protection. Even on a cloudy or hazy day the sun rays can penetrate up to 80%. Radiation from the sun can even penetrate thru the windows in your car, so consider them having them tinted with a protective UV film.

Tip 5: Stay away from tanning salons! The UV light emitted from these tanning beds are even more intense than natural sun light.

Tip 6: and finally remember to practice skin self-examination at least every three months. If you spot anything suspicious, see a doctor immediately

<u>SPEECH TOPICS</u>

Speech Topic: ATHLETES

General Goal _____

Specific Goal _____

Thesis Statement _____

_____

_____

Introduction:

Body:

Conclusion:

Work Cited:

Speech Topic: PERFORMANCE ENHANCING DRUGS

General Goal _____

Specific Goal _____

Thesis Statement _____

_____

_____

Introduction:

Body:

Conclusion:

Work Cited:

Speech Topic: JUVENILE STREET GANGS

General Goal _____

Specific Goal _____

Thesis Statement _____

_____

_____

Introduction:

Body:

Conclusion:

Work Cited:

Speech Topic: AIR FORCE PILOTS

General Goal _____

Specific Goal _____

Thesis Statement _____

_____

_____

Introduction:

Body:

Conclusion:

Work Cited:

Speech Topic: MEDIA RESPONSIBILITY

General Goal _____

Specific Goal _____

Thesis Statement _____

_____

_____

Introduction:

Body:

Conclusion:

Work Cited:

Speech Topic: JOURNALISM

General Goal _____

Specific Goal _____

Thesis Statement _____

_____

_____

Introduction:

Body:

Conclusion:

Work Cited:

Speech Topic: SECOND HAND SMOKE

General Goal _____

Specific Goal _____

Thesis Statement _____

_____

_____

Introduction:

Body:

Conclusion:

Work Cited:

Speech Topic: SPORTSMANSHIP

General Goal _____

Specific Goal _____

Thesis Statement _____

_____

_____

Introduction:

Body:

Conclusion:

Work Cited:

Speech Topic: BASEBALL PLAYERS SALARY CAP

General Goal _____

Specific Goal _____

Thesis Statement _____

_____

_____

Introduction:

Body:

Conclusion:

Work Cited:

Speech Topic: FEMINISM

General Goal _____

Specific Goal _____

Thesis Statement _____

_____

_____

Introduction:

Body:

Conclusion:

Work Cited:

Speech Topic: MILITARY LIFE

General Goal _____

Specific Goal _____

Thesis Statement _____
_____
_____

Introduction:

Body:

Conclusion:

Work Cited:

Speech Topic: HOW TO PLAY A GUITER

General Goal _____

Specific Goal _____

Thesis Statement _____

_____

_____

Introduction:

Body:

Conclusion:

Work Cited:

Speech Topic: HOW TO PLAY A PIANO

General Goal _____

Specific Goal _____

Thesis Statement _____

_____

_____

Introduction:

Body:

Conclusion:

Work Cited:

Speech Topic: ORGAN TRANSPLANT

General Goal _____

Specific Goal _____

Thesis Statement _____

_____

_____

Introduction:

Body:

Conclusion:

Work Cited:

Speech Topic: ART

General Goal _____

Specific Goal _____

Thesis Statement _____

_____

_____

Introduction:

Body:

Conclusion:

Work Cited:

Speech Topic: THE GRAND CANYON

General Goal _____

Specific Goal _____

Thesis Statement _____

_____

_____

Introduction:

Body:

Conclusion:

Work Cited:

Speech Topic: FOOD STAMPS

General Goal _____

Specific Goal _____

Thesis Statement _____

_____

_____

Introduction:

Body:

Conclusion:

Work Cited:

Speech Topic: PLAGIARISM

General Goal _____

Specific Goal _____

Thesis Statement _____

_____

_____

Introduction:

Body:

Conclusion:

Work Cited:

Speech Topic: CAR INSURANCE

General Goal _____

Specific Goal _____

Thesis Statement _____

_____

_____

Introduction:

Body:

Conclusion:

Work Cited:

Speech Topic: WORK STUDY PROGRAMS

General Goal _____

Specific Goal _____

Thesis Statement _____

_____

_____

Introduction:

Body:

Conclusion:

Work Cited:

Speech Topic: DINOSAURS

General Goal _____

Specific Goal _____

Thesis Statement _____

_____

_____

Introduction:

Body:

Conclusion:

Work Cited:

Speech Topic: HOW TO IMPROVE YOUR RELATIONSHIP

General Goal _____

Specific Goal _____

Thesis Statement _____

_____

_____

Introduction:

Body:

Conclusion:

Work Cited:

Speech Topic: CONFLICT RESOLUTION STYLES

General Goal _____

Specific Goal _____

Thesis Statement _____

_____

_____

Introduction:

Body:

Conclusion:

Work Cited:

Speech Topic: CAMPAIGN FUNDS

General Goal _____

Specific Goal _____

Thesis Statement _____

_____

_____

Introduction:

Body:

Conclusion:

Work Cited:

Speech Topic: HOW TO BAKE MONKEY BREAD

General Goal _____

Specific Goal _____

Thesis Statement _____

_____

_____

Introduction:

Body:

Conclusion:

Work Cited:

Speech Topic: HOW TO BAKE CAKE COOKIES

General Goal _____

Specific Goal _____

Thesis Statement _____

_____

_____

Introduction:

Body:

Conclusion:

Work Cited:

Speech Topic: BASEBALL

General Goal _____

Specific Goal _____

Thesis Statement _____

_____

_____

Introduction:

Body:

Conclusion:

Work Cited:

Speech Topic: BASKETBALL

General Goal _____

Specific Goal _____

Thesis Statement _____

_____

_____

Introduction:

Body:

Conclusion:

Work Cited:

Speech Topic: THE GAME OF FOOTBALL

General Goal _____

Specific Goal _____

Thesis Statement _____

_____

_____

Introduction:

Body:

Conclusion:

Work Cited:

Speech Topic: SOCCER

General Goal _____

Specific Goal _____

Thesis Statement _____

_____

_____

Introduction:

Body:

Conclusion:

Work Cited:

Speech Topic: FIRE SAFETY

General Goal _____

Specific Goal _____

Thesis Statement _____

_____

_____

Introduction:

Body:

Conclusion:

Work Cited:

Speech Topic: MASSAGE THERAPY

General Goal _____

Specific Goal _____

Thesis Statement _____

_____

_____

Introduction:

Body:

Conclusion:

Work Cited:

Speech Topic: REALITY TELEVISION SHOWS

General Goal _____

Specific Goal _____

Thesis Statement _____

_____

_____

Introduction:

Body:

Conclusion:

Work Cited:

Speech Topic: ACUPRESSURE

General Goal _____

Specific Goal _____

Thesis Statement _____

_____

_____

Introduction:

Body:

Conclusion:

Work Cited:

Speech Topic: HOMEOPATHY

General Goal _____

Specific Goal _____

Thesis Statement _____

_____

_____

Introduction:

Body:

Conclusion:

Work Cited:

Speech Topic: CHIROPRACTICE

General Goal _____

Specific Goal _____

Thesis Statement _____

_____

_____

Introduction:

Body:

Conclusion:

Work Cited:

Speech Topic: GARDENING

General Goal _____

Specific Goal _____

Thesis Statement _____

_____

_____

Introduction:

Body:

Conclusion:

Work Cited:

Speech Topic: THRASH COLLECTION
   BUSINESS

General Goal _____

Specific Goal _____

Thesis Statement _____

_____

_____

Introduction:

Body:

Conclusion:

Work Cited:

Speech Topic: JOURNALISM

General Goal _____
Specific Goal _____
Thesis Statement _____
_____
_____

Introduction:

Body:

Conclusion:

Work Cited:

Speech Topic: WATER POLLUTION

General Goal _____

Specific Goal _____

Thesis Statement _____

_____

_____

Introduction:

Body:

Conclusion:

Work Cited:

Speech Topic: EARTH POLLUTION

General Goal _____

Specific Goal _____

Thesis Statement _____

_____

_____

Introduction:

Body:

Conclusion:

Work Cited:

Speech Topic: AIR POLLUTION

General Goal _____

Specific Goal _____

Thesis Statement _____

_____

_____

Introduction:

Body:

Conclusion:

Work Cited:

Speech Topic: CANCER

General Goal _____

Specific Goal _____

Thesis Statement _____

_____

_____

Introduction:

Body:

Conclusion:

Work Cited:

Speech Topic: CREDIT CARD FRAUD

General Goal _____

Specific Goal _____

Thesis Statement _____

_____

_____

Introduction:

Body:

Conclusion:

Work Cited:

Speech Topic: CANCER TREATMENT

General Goal _____

Specific Goal _____

Thesis Statement _____

_____

_____

Introduction:

Body:

Conclusion:

Work Cited:

Speech Topic: FINANCIAL AIDS

General Goal _____

Specific Goal _____

Thesis Statement _____

_____

_____

Introduction:

Body:

Conclusion:

Work Cited:

Speech Topic: REVERSE DISCRIMINATION

General Goal _____

Specific Goal _____

Thesis Statement _____

_____

_____

Introduction:

Body:

Conclusion:

Work Cited:

Speech Topic: HOW THE BRAIN FUNCTION

General Goal _____

Specific Goal _____

Thesis Statement _____

_____

_____

Introduction:

Body:

Conclusion:

Work Cited:

Speech Topic: FOSTER HOMES

General Goal _____

Specific Goal _____

Thesis Statement _____

_____

_____

Introduction:

Body:

Conclusion:

Work Cited:

Speech Topic: HOW TO BE A MENTOR

General Goal _____

Specific Goal _____

Thesis Statement _____

_____

_____

Introduction:

Body:

Conclusion:

Work Cited:

Speech Topic: EXCHANGE STUDENTS PROGRAM

General Goal _____

Specific Goal _____

Thesis Statement _____

_____

_____

Introduction:

Body:

Conclusion:

Work Cited:

Speech Topic: ALZHEIMER

General Goal _____

Specific Goal _____

Thesis Statement _____

_____

_____

Introduction:

Body:

Conclusion:

Work Cited:

Speech Topic: SOLAR ENERGY

General Goal _____

Specific Goal _____

Thesis Statement _____

_____

_____

Introduction:

Body:

Conclusion:

Work Cited:

Speech Topic: LIGUID GAS

General Goal _____

Specific Goal _____

Thesis Statement _____

_____

_____

Introduction:

Body:

Conclusion:

Work Cited:

Speech Topic: PET THERAPHY

General Goal _____

Specific Goal _____

Thesis Statement _____

_____

_____

Introduction:

Body:

Conclusion:

Work Cited:

Speech Topic: HOW TO FILE FOR
    BANKRUPTCY

General Goal _____

Specific Goal _____

Thesis Statement _____

                  _____

                  _____

Introduction:

Body:

Conclusion:

Work Cited:

Speech Topic: HOW TO CHOOSE A CAREER

General Goal _____

Specific Goal _____

Thesis Statement _____

_____

_____

Introduction:

Body:

Conclusion:

Work Cited:

Speech Topic: DANGERS OF SCHOOL VOUCHERS

General Goal _____

Specific Goal _____

Thesis Statement _____

_____

_____

Introduction:

Body:

Conclusion:

Work Cited:

Speech Topic: EDUCATIONAL STANDARDS OF
   COMMUNITY COLLEGES

General Goal _____
Specific Goal _____
Thesis Statement _____
   _____
   _____

Introduction:

Body:

Conclusion:

Work Cited:

Speech Topic: HOW TO IMPROVE FAMILY RELATIONSHIPS

General Goal _____

Specific Goal _____

Thesis Statement _____

_____

_____

Introduction:

Body:

Conclusion:

Work Cited:

Speech Topic: DATING

General Goal _____

Specific Goal _____

Thesis Statement _____

_____

_____

Introduction:

Body:

Conclusion:

Work Cited:

Speech Topic: CREATIVE WRITING

General Goal _____

Specific Goal _____

Thesis Statement _____

_____

_____

Introduction:

Body:

Conclusion:

Work Cited:

Speech Topic: HOW TECHNOLOGY AFFECTS
   HUMAN COMMUNICATION

General Goal _____

Specific Goal _____

Thesis Statement _____

   _____

   _____

Introduction:

Body:

Conclusion:

Work Cited:

Speech Topic: DEATH PENALTY

General Goal _____

Specific Goal _____

Thesis Statement _____

_____

_____

Introduction:

Body:

Conclusion:

Work Cited:

Speech Topic: DIABETES AND DIET

General Goal _____

Specific Goal _____

Thesis Statement _____

_____

_____

Introduction:

Body:

Conclusion:

Work Cited:

Speech Topic: CLASSICAL MUSIC

General Goal _____

Specific Goal _____

Thesis Statement _____

_____

_____

Introduction:

Body:

Conclusion:

Work Cited:

Speech Topic: MUSIC IN THE 12TH CENTURY

General Goal _____

Specific Goal _____

Thesis Statement _____

_____

_____

Introduction:

Body:

Conclusion:

Work Cited:

Speech Topic: MUSIC IN THE 19TH CENTURY

General Goal _____

Specific Goal _____

Thesis Statement _____

_____

_____

Introduction:

Body:

Conclusion:

Work Cited:

Speech Topic: COUNTRY MUSIC

General Goal _____

Specific Goal _____

Thesis Statement _____

_____

_____

Introduction:

Body:

Conclusion:

Work Cited:

Speech Topic: RAP MUSIC

General Goal _____

Specific Goal _____

Thesis Statement _____

_____

_____

Introduction:

Body:

Conclusion:

Work Cited:

Speech Topic: MUSIC AND VIOLENCE

General Goal _____

Specific Goal _____

Thesis Statement _____

_____

_____

Introduction:

Body:

Conclusion:

Work Cited:

Speech Topic: MEDIA AND SEX

General Goal _____

Specific Goal _____

Thesis Statement _____

_____

_____

Introduction:

Body:

Conclusion:

Work Cited:

Speech Topic: INTERACIAL ADOPTION

General Goal _____

Specific Goal _____

Thesis Statement _____

_____

_____

Introduction:

Body:

Conclusion:

Work Cited:

Speech Topic: WOMEN AND CARDINAL
    ORDINATION

General Goal _____
Specific Goal _____
Thesis Statement _____
    _____
    _____

Introduction:

Body:

Conclusion:

Work Cited:

Speech Topic: AFFIRMATIVE ACTION

General Goal _____

Specific Goal _____

Thesis Statement _____

_____

_____

Introduction:

Body:

Conclusion:

Work Cited:

Speech Topic: HOW TO START A SMALL BUSINESS

General Goal _____

Specific Goal _____

Thesis Statement _____

_____

_____

Introduction:

Body:

Conclusion:

Work Cited:

Speech Topic: INTERACIAL MARRIAGE

General Goal _____

Specific Goal _____

Thesis Statement _____

_____

_____

Introduction:

Body:

Conclusion:

Work Cited:

Speech Topic: INTERACIAL DATING

General Goal _____

Specific Goal _____

Thesis Statement _____

_____

_____

Introduction:

Body:

Conclusion:

Work Cited:

Speech Topic: PRE-MARITAL SEX

General Goal _____

Specific Goal _____

Thesis Statement _____

_____

_____

Introduction:

Body:

Conclusion:

Work Cited:

Speech Topic: POLITICAL PROPOGANDA

General Goal _____

Specific Goal _____

Thesis Statement _____

_____

_____

Introduction:

Body:

Conclusion:

Work Cited:

Speech Topic: ETHICS IN AMERICA

General Goal _____

Specific Goal _____

Thesis Statement _____

_____

_____

Introduction:

Body:

Conclusion:

Work Cited:

Speech Topic: HOW TO INTERPRETE THE STOCK MARKET

General Goal _____

Specific Goal _____

Thesis Statement _____

_____

_____

Introduction:

Body:

Conclusion:

Work Cited:

Speech Topic: DIPLOMATIC IMMUNITY

General Goal _____

Specific Goal _____

Thesis Statement _____

_____

_____

Introduction:

Body:

Conclusion:

Work Cited:

Speech Topic: MEDICAL LAWSUIT CAP

General Goal _____

Specific Goal _____

Thesis Statement _____

_____

_____

Introduction:

Body:

Conclusion:

Work Cited:

Speech Topic: DOCTOR-PATIENT
  RELATIONSHIP

General Goal _____
Specific Goal _____
Thesis Statement _____
  _____
  _____

Introduction:

Body:

Conclusion:

Work Cited:

Speech Topic: GENERIC DRUGS VERSUS NAME BRAND

General Goal _____

Specific Goal _____

Thesis Statement _____

_____

_____

Introduction:

Body:

Conclusion:

Work Cited:

Speech Topic: AGE DIFFERENCES IN CULTURE

General Goal _____

Specific Goal _____

Thesis Statement _____

_____

_____

Introduction:

Body:

Conclusion:

Work Cited:

Speech Topic: IMMIGRATION IN AMERICA

General Goal _____

Specific Goal _____

Thesis Statement _____

_____

_____

Introduction:

Body:

Conclusion:

Work Cited:

Speech Topic: HOSPITAL COST FOR IMMIGRANTS IN AMERICA

General Goal _____

Specific Goal _____

Thesis Statement _____

_____

_____

Introduction:

Body:

Conclusion:

Work Cited:

Speech Topic: MEDICAL MALPRACTICE

General Goal _____

Specific Goal _____

Thesis Statement _____

_____

_____

Introduction:

Body:

Conclusion:

Work Cited:

Speech Topic: COMPUTER GAMES

General Goal _____

Specific Goal _____

Thesis Statement _____

_____

_____

Introduction:

Body:

Conclusion:

Work Cited:

Speech Topic: COMPUTER SOFTWARES

General Goal _____

Specific Goal _____

Thesis Statement _____

_____

_____

Introduction:

Body:

Conclusion:

Work Cited:

Speech Topic: HOW TO PREVENT COMPUTER
    VIRUS

General Goal _____

Specific Goal _____

Thesis Statement _____

                      _____

                      _____

Introduction:

Body:

Conclusion:

Work Cited:

Speech Topic: HOW TO DOWNLOAD A
   DOCUMENT ON YOUR COMPUTER

General Goal _____
Specific Goal _____
Thesis Statement _____
                           _____
                           _____

Introduction:

Body:

Conclusion:

Work Cited:

Speech Topic: HOW TO INCREASE YOUR LIFESPAN

General Goal _____

Specific Goal _____

Thesis Statement _____

_____

_____

Introduction:

Body:

Conclusion:

Work Cited:

Speech Topic: HOLISTIC MEDICINES

General Goal _____

Specific Goal _____

Thesis Statement _____

_____

_____

Introduction:

Body:

Conclusion:

Work Cited:

Speech Topic: RICKY WILLIAMS

General Goal _____

Specific Goal _____

Thesis Statement _____

_____

_____

Introduction:

Body:

Conclusion:

Work Cited:

Speech Topic: MUSCLE GROWTH

General Goal _____

Specific Goal _____

Thesis Statement _____

_____

_____

Introduction:

Body:

Conclusion:

Work Cited:

Speech Topic: HOW TO PREPARE FOR AN EXAM

General Goal _____

Specific Goal _____

Thesis Statement _____

_____

_____

Introduction:

Body:

Conclusion:

Work Cited:

Speech Topic: PERSONALITY DISORDER

General Goal _____

Specific Goal _____

Thesis Statement _____

_____

_____

Introduction:

Body:

Conclusion:

Work Cited:

Speech Topic: GOTHIC

General Goal _____

Specific Goal _____

Thesis Statement _____

_____

_____

Introduction:

Body:

Conclusion:

Work Cited:

Speech Topic: HOW CULTURE AFFECTS THE WAY WE COMMUNICATE WITH OTHERS

General Goal _____

Specific Goal _____

Thesis Statement _____

_____

_____

Introduction:

Body:

Conclusion:

Work Cited:

Speech Topic: ANCIENT ARCHITECTURE AND
   MATHEMATICS

General Goal _____

Specific Goal _____

Thesis Statement _____

_____

_____

Introduction:

Body:

Conclusion:

Work Cited:

Speech Topic: THE ROLE OF SCIENCE IN
      TODAYS SOCIETY

General Goal _____

Specific Goal _____

Thesis Statement _____

              _____

              _____

Introduction:

Body:

Conclusion:

Work Cited:

Speech Topic: WIND ENERGY AND THE FUTURE OF AERONAUTIC ENGINEERING

General Goal _____

Specific Goal _____

Thesis Statement _____

_____

_____

Introduction:

Body:

Conclusion:

Work Cited:

Speech Topic: GREEK PHILOSOPHY

General Goal _____

Specific Goal _____

Thesis Statement _____

_____

_____

Introduction:

Body:

Conclusion:

Work Cited:

Speech Topic: FISHING

General Goal _____

Specific Goal _____

Thesis Statement _____

_____

_____

Introduction:

Body:

Conclusion:

Work Cited:

Speech Topic: HOW TO COOK FISH FOR DINNER

General Goal _____

Specific Goal _____

Thesis Statement _____

_____

_____

Introduction:

Body:

Conclusion:

Work Cited:

Speech Topic: EGYPTIAN PAINTING AND
  CODES

General Goal _____

Specific Goal _____

Thesis Statement _____

_____

_____

Introduction:

Body:

Conclusion:

Work Cited:

Speech Topic: THE F.B. I

General Goal _____

Specific Goal _____

Thesis Statement _____

_____

_____

Introduction:

Body:

Conclusion:

Work Cited:

Speech Topic: AFIRCAN RELIGIONS

General Goal _____

Specific Goal _____

Thesis Statement _____

_____

_____

Introduction:

Body:

Conclusion:

Work Cited:

Speech Topic: WALL STREET GLADIATORS

General Goal _____

Specific Goal _____

Thesis Statement _____

_____

_____

Introduction:

Body:

Conclusion:

Work Cited:

Speech Topic: DIFFERENT VIEWS OF
   EVOLUTION

General Goal _____

Specific Goal _____

Thesis Statement _____

   _____

   _____

Introduction:

Body:

Conclusion:

Work Cited:

Speech Topic: FUNERAL RITUALS IN RUSSIA

General Goal _____

Specific Goal _____

Thesis Statement _____

_____

_____

Introduction:

Body:

Conclusion:

Work Cited:

Speech Topic: EFFECTS OF EARTHQUAKES

General Goal _____

Specific Goal _____

Thesis Statement _____

_____

_____

Introduction:

Body:

Conclusion:

Work Cited:

Speech Topic: SELF DEFENCE

General Goal _____

Specific Goal _____

Thesis Statement _____

_____

_____

Introduction:

Body:

Conclusion:

Work Cited:

Speech Topic: HYPNOTISM

General Goal _____

Specific Goal _____

Thesis Statement _____

_____

_____

Introduction:

Body:

Conclusion:

Work Cited:

Speech Topic: MODERN MEDICINE AND HERBS

General Goal _____

Specific Goal _____

Thesis Statement _____

_____

_____

Introduction:

Body:

Conclusion:

Work Cited:

Speech Topic: HOW TO INSTALL A SMOKE
   DETECTOR

General Goal _____

Specific Goal _____

Thesis Statement _____

_____

_____

Introduction:

Body:

Conclusion:

Work Cited:

Speech Topic: HOW TO BECOME A POLICE OFFICER

General Goal _____

Specific Goal _____

Thesis Statement _____

_____

_____

Introduction:

Body:

Conclusion:

Work Cited:

Speech Topic: KLEPTOMANIA

General Goal _____

Specific Goal _____

Thesis Statement _____

_____

_____

Introduction:

Body:

Conclusion:

Work Cited:

Speech Topic: AIDS

General Goal _____
Specific Goal _____
Thesis Statement _____
_____
_____

Introduction:

Body:

Conclusion:

Work Cited:

Speech Topic: ADHD

General Goal _____
Specific Goal _____
Thesis Statement _____
_____
_____

Introduction:

Body:

Conclusion:

Work Cited:

Speech Topic: SYMPTOMS OF ADHD

General Goal _____

Specific Goal _____

Thesis Statement _____

_____

_____

Introduction:

Body:

Conclusion:

Work Cited:

Speech Topic: PRISON REFORMS

General Goal _____

Specific Goal _____

Thesis Statement _____

_____

_____

Introduction:

Body:

Conclusion:

Work Cited:

Speech Topic: HISTORY OF PRISONS

General Goal _____

Specific Goal _____

Thesis Statement _____

_____

_____

Introduction:

Body:

Conclusion:

Work Cited:

Speech Topic: HOW TO BUILD A HOUSE

General Goal _____

Specific Goal _____

Thesis Statement _____

_____

_____

Introduction:

Body:

Conclusion:

Work Cited:

Speech Topic: NASA

General Goal _____
Specific Goal _____
Thesis Statement _____
_____
_____

Introduction:

Body:

Conclusion:

Work Cited:

Speech Topic: RING TONES

General Goal _____

Specific Goal _____

Thesis Statement _____

_____

_____

Introduction:

Body:

Conclusion:

Work Cited:

Speech Topic: HAZARDS OF CELLPHONES

General Goal _____

Specific Goal _____

Thesis Statement _____

_____

_____

Introduction:

Body:

Conclusion:

Work Cited:

Speech Topic: IDENTITY THEFT

General Goal _____

Specific Goal _____

Thesis Statement _____

_____

_____

Introduction:

Body:

Conclusion:

Work Cited:

Speech Topic: SEVEN WONDERS OF THE WORLD

General Goal _____

Specific Goal _____

Thesis Statement _____

_____

_____

Introduction:

Body:

Conclusion:

Work Cited:

Speech Topic: EFFECTS OF CAFFEINE

General Goal _____

Specific Goal _____

Thesis Statement _____

_____

_____

Introduction:

Body:

Conclusion:

Work Cited:

Speech Topic: VIOLENCE AND THE MEDIA

General Goal _____

Specific Goal _____

Thesis Statement _____

_____

_____

Introduction:

Body:

Conclusion:

Work Cited:

Speech Topic: ART COLLECTION

General Goal _____

Specific Goal _____

Thesis Statement _____

_____

_____

Introduction:

Body:

Conclusion:

Work Cited:

Speech Topic: CANCER CELLS

General Goal _____

Specific Goal _____

Thesis Statement _____

_____

_____

Introduction:

Body:

Conclusion:

Work Cited:

Speech Topic: POVERTY

General Goal _____

Specific Goal _____

Thesis Statement _____

_____

_____

Introduction:

Body:

Conclusion:

Work Cited:

Speech Topic: DIET

General Goal _____

Specific Goal _____

Thesis Statement _____

_____

_____

Introduction:

Body:

Conclusion:

Work Cited:

Speech Topic: CANNED FOODS AND CANCER

General Goal _____

Specific Goal _____

Thesis Statement _____

_____

_____

Introduction:

Body:

Conclusion:

Work Cited:

Speech Topic: JURY SELECTION

General Goal _____

Specific Goal _____

Thesis Statement _____

_____

_____

Introduction:

Body:

Conclusion:

Work Cited:

Speech Topic: JURY DUTY

General Goal _____

Specific Goal _____

Thesis Statement _____

_____

_____

Introduction:

Body:

Conclusion:

Work Cited: